Fluent Thoughts©

The Journey Of A Bird: Volume One

By Hussein Farah

ISBN: 978-1-291-63927-8

For enquires contact the author: Husseinfarah@me.com
Twitter: Fluentthought

ISBN: 978-1-291-63927-

Contents

Dedication

For every bird that seeks to be free in spirit and aspires to excel in everything they do in life.

Preface

In my late teens, expressive writing became a personal tool to pour out my thoughts, feelings and aspirations on paper. I continued to do so into my early twenties when a life changing event, in my college year, widened my eyes. I recall the incident vividly, it was during a reading session where my English teacher began to shed tears in front of the whole class after reading a poem I had written. She then questioned me as to whether I had read any books or if someone had taught me to write so deeply and creatively. I informed her that I learned the art through my own initiative as I have had the urge and desire to express my innermost feelings since childhood. Consequently, she selected me to attend a political event, centred on the youth vote, at the college campus.

Since that day on, I began to believe that I had the gift of expression but I wasn't sure if I could make something out of it. As time passed, I shared my private work with a number of people, from friends and family to a university lecturer, who were all moved by my imagination and creativity. The lecturer insisted that I should pursue a career in writing, while friends and family held me in a high regard. The praise and admiration continued to pour in, which overwhelmed me but I remained doubtful of having a career in the field of authorship.

Thereafter, I discovered that I had accumulated a large body of work; thanks to the years of honing my writing skills coupled with an innate ability to perceive, comprehend and translate what I felt, learned and imagined. The latter blessing enabled me to write a variety of material, from fictional stories to philosophical poems, without difficulty.

And so, I finally decided to take on writing as a career because I came to see and believe that I have a natural talent with pen and paper in hand. Expressive writing, whether philosophical or fiction, is my destiny and a God given talent that I choose to pursue. With this book title I aim to share my story telling and poetic work.

Prologue

Life is one big road with traffic, junctions, bumps, road signs and all the weather that comes with it. It is a journey to the unknown future through the known present and rear view past.

Fluent Thoughts is a poetic story of a birds journey in life, from its emancipation, to its redemption, affection, comprehension, and message. I hope you enjoy it as much as I enjoy dreaming and writing.

Acknowledgments

Many thanks to friends and family who were either editors, reviewers, listeners or they were simply rooting for me to put a book together. I am also thankful for the gift of life which gave me the experience to write my vision, thoughts and feelings.

Nimo Ali
Olu Awoyemi
John Bamidele
Naaj Bourgeoisie
Oluwatosin Dada
Oyewole John Esan
Abdi Aziz Farah
Jodi-Ann Forbes
David Ibiaye
Asha Jama
Victor (Mr Jayvic) Johnson
Wahid Islam Mahdi
Idan Naor
Kivumba Nkone
Aaron Okoro (Editor)
Munira Waheed

The Beginning

The Bird In The Cage

In this technological age
The human race
Is locked up in a cage
Caught up in a chase
Reputation is the gauge
So the bird is trapped in a maze
Lifelong insecurities cripples rage
The predator controls the place
A common tool in history's page
Regulating the breathing space
So the mind is unable to disengage
Domination dictates the pace
Acceptance is the first stage
Lost & confused with a poker face
Total obedience for a living wage
While mental slavery is big a disgrace
The bird brags on of being a sage.

Bird Is Advised

Brown Sugar

Do you think you have tasted sweet?
Not until you've been swept off your feet
Processed things can turn you weak
But the pure stuff makes your health peak
So check the difference with taste and feel
Because anything can sell as real
Once you try it you'll turn to freshly cool
And wonder why the old made you drool
So pick up the authentic for your living basket
Before you leave this world in a wishing casket
The good things in life turns you manic
Simply because brown sugar is organic.

Bird Reads A Story

The sheep that broke free

There was once a sheep born into a family of sheep, it grew up to know and admire the group. Whatever they did she did, wherever they went she went; she lived under the cover and warmth of the herd.

One day she asked another young sheep, '*Have you ever wondered why we sheep huddle together in one spot?*'

'*It's safe, warm and who wants to be alone?,*' The other sheep replied. Whenever she tried to step out from the group, they would turn with judging eyes.

'*Why would she do that? Is she stupid? She is weird! Does she want to be eaten by the wolves?,*' She would hear.

When she took a step back in the group they praised and complimented her. She felt loved and special but she was terrified to be herself because nobody would love her for her. Years had passed and she could not help but wonder what the purpose of life was, something was missing and she felt empty. Her curiosity turned to dreams, deep down she had this urge to find out what her purpose was. The sheep wondered what life would be like on the other side of the world but was she ready to lose all the love? Was she ready to be alone? Could she face the bitter cold? Would she survive alone if she came across the wolves ?

'What is the point of living if I am waking up every day to the same thing?,' She thought to herself.

With bravely, she stepped out from the group even though they gave her the looks, ridiculed her and warned her that she will be taken by the wolves. She kept on walking even though she was afraid, and she never looked back even when the feeling of loneliness dawned on her. She faced her fears because deep down she felt she was doing the right thing. She knew being herself mattered more than anything else and she was ready to die for something than live for nothing.

As she was strolling through the wilderness, she stumbled into three hungry wolves. One of the wolves began laughing loudly, and the others joined in.

'This is the easiest catch of our lives,' one wolf said.

The sheep was fearful at first but she realised that she decided to die for what she believed in. Then suddenly, she violently charged towards one of the wolves and it moved aside before being struck by the sheep. The young defiant sheep ended up crashing head first into a rocky mountain. With a bloodied face, she turned to charge at the wolves once more and the wolves turned to look at themselves with amazement.

'This one is crazy, I've never seen a fearless sheep before,' One wolf said.

'I think if we eat it we will catch some kind of illness,' Another replied.

And so the wolves walked away and disappeared into the distance.

The sheep could not believe what had just happened, they've always been on the run when the wolves chased the herd but today the carnivores walked away from one lone sheep. From that day on the sheep believed she could face anything that came her way. While her group was at a standstill, she took big leap forward into her destiny and so the young sheep took the world by storm.

Years had passed since she left the group, the herd excused her departure as stupidity and they believed she was long dead.
One day the sheep returned to her motherland, she had changed beyond recognition. The herd were in shock to discover she was alive and well with her family accompanying her. She spoke of the adventures she had, the people she met and the places she visited around the world. She told the tale of the three wolves she encountered with a visible scar across her face as proof to the attentive listeners . The herd couldn't help but feel so stupid and ashamed, they turned and looked at themselves.

'what have we been doing all these years?,' The herd thought to themselves.

The group broke into tears and hugged the sheep, pleading for forgiveness for the ill treatment she received. And so they came to admire her for her strength, they were inspired by her courage and they came to love her for who she was. Wherever she went they followed and whatever she did they copied, she went from the little sheep to the Queen of the herd.

In the end, she kindly requested the herd to find something worth dying for or life would be meaningless. Consequently, one hundred sheep took on 20 strong packs of wolves and the beasts dashed out of their grazing area for the first time in their lives. This is the tale of a legendary sheep who broke free to take on her destiny.

Bird Is In Denial

The Truth

The truth may be immense
But ignorance is no defence
Honesty has us up against the fence
But hiding from self is a difficult suspense
As time passes with the false pretence
The heavy burden will get intense
Confronting reality makes sense
Because your sanity is the expense
So wake up, live up and take no offence.

Bird Seeks Freedom

Free Spirit

The quest for emancipation
Begins with the spirits elevation
So free self from life's limitations
and the habit of procrastination
Avoid the forces of suffocation
Such as the infectious tribulations
The frantic frustrations
The blind dramatisations
Societies sophistications
The taunting provocations
The ignorance of discrimination
The absence of motivation
And emotional domination
This is spiritual liberation
And a living existence through simplification
Be a free bird with positive aspirations.

The Dreaming Bird

Dreams do come true

When you believe in you
Surround yourself with a close few
If you want your dreams to come true
Make sure those around you have a clue
Some don't see it in them
So how could they see you as a gem?
You need those who hear you out
Not those who give you doubt
Today you may be on a low
Still push forward and watch your seeds grow
The sky is the limit so jump high
Then spread your wings and fly
Impossible as it may seem
Reality is made out of dreams.

Bird On A Journey

Road To Glory

The road to glory begins with the ignition
So start the engine and take up a mission
The road to glory is a mountain climbing venture
So get ready for the adventure
The road to glory will have countless signs
So heed the warnings before you take on fines
The road to glory is known to have foggy mists
So focus your vision and persist
The road to glory may be bumpy and rough
So strap on your seat belt and remain tough
The road to glory will have countless confusions
So use your mind and see past the illusions
The road to glory will ground you with broken wings
But do you know that ordinary men became Kings?

The Emotional Bird

Queen of Hearts

The heart coordinates the emotions traffic
It guides us through the world's geographic
When the signal turns bright green
It means go ahead and explore the scene
When the signal turns to amber flash
It means proceed with caution and don't be rash
When the signal turns to an alarming red
It means stop, wait and use your head
So let the king of genius reason and decide
And the queen of hearts feel and guide.

The Bird's Love Encounter

Summer Breeze

The picture of perfection
Mesmerised by feelings of affection
As I turned with a glance
I was captured with a hypnotic trance
You flicked your hair with a teasing dare
And I couldn't help the eternal stare
Suddenly you disappeared into the distance
So I chased you up with persistence
Then and there I knew it was meant to be
A future together I hoped you'd agree
I grabbed you by your hands
And I asked you to hear out my plans
As we began to converse
The feelings of chemistry began to immerse
It felt like nobody else mattered
I complimented your looks, and you said, '*I am flattered*'
We sat down and spoke
The unforgettable moment of how we shared a coke
In the moment of silence, you looked away
Speechless, we had little words to say

Then suddenly we locked eyes
And our heart rates shot up to new highs
So I pulled you next to me
I did so respectfully
I grabbed you and hugged you up close
with my hands holding your hips like I would a rose
The desire to touch lips makes one lose control
And so passionate kisses connected our souls
We locked lips with our eyes closed
The tunes of tremble our bodies composed
You whispered, '*Hug me good, love me good, never hurt me nor desert me*'
I softly replied, '*if you'll be my queen, I won't let anything come in between. I won't deceive you nor leave you, and If my gun shoots life, it's God's gift to the womb of a wife*'
Nothing else matters in time freeze
It was written that you'd be my summer breeze.

Gun In A Holster

A man's gun is his leisure
Mankind's creation treasure
A man's gun goes through transformation
An aphrodisiac designed for exploration
A man's gun yearns for pleasure
Scanning eyes judges its measure
A man's gun becomes his identity
Displayed in acts of obscenity
A man's gun infected with greed
Demoralises souls as broken hearts bleed
A man's gun seeks lust
Deceiving practices kills trust
A man's gun evokes fears
Those with past scars remember the tears
A man's gun was crafted to shoot life
God's gift to the womb of a wife
A man's gun belongs in a holster
Those who keep it for a Queen are true soldiers.

The Pretence Of Money

Money buy's all you want
Fancy dresses with matching shoes
Flashy cars for all to see
A cosy home to lazy in.
A lover of your dreams
A bunch of friends to celebrate with
The stories told are so sweet
And adventures taken are a treat

You are convinced of happiness
But something within is gone astray
With all the possessions all the crowds
Still the soul feels so foul
Eternal joy has no price
Something you just realised

The misery is masked
With a smile on your face
And tears fall behind closed doors
The loud laughs covers the pain

And items bought heals the sorrow
The bonds made are falsely hollow
So voices within questioned tomorrow

'*How lucky you are,*' people say
So count your blessings as you pray
The bed you made is where you lay
A comfort worth it so you stay
With an empty soul you act brave
A truth untold forever a slave
So money's pretence becomes your grave.

Bird Hears A Story

Jungled Up

There was once a boy who left his village to make it big in the cities. He moved up the ranks in the biggest organisations but he did so by playing the game to win. After a few years he earned what he desired; the cars, the chick, the crib and the top spot as the CEO. So he revisited his village where they all embraced him after his long absence.

Within a few days, the elder Chief gathered the villagers for a meeting. He reported that he received numerous complaints regarding the boy's attitude. His people insisted that the boy had changed internally, they all agreed that there was something different about him. He only greeted a select few when he passed, he made funny faces when some sat next to him, he spoke over people with disregard, and he had an awkward silence with shunning eyes. The father reported to the chief that he had raised his voice towards his mother, when she grabbed his expensive belongings, and he expressed his disgust for the food they ate.

The Chief told the villagers a story of a boy who was lost in the wilderness. The boy was found five years later, unable to talk, walk upright and he had not bathed at all. He became consumed by his surroundings and he behaved like his adoptive parents. The boy was known as Lost Boy as he was raised by animals in the jungle.

The Chief told his people that the current boy is a product of his environment, he behaves like Lost Boy but worse. One villager asked the chief why their rich boy would behave in such a manner, since in the modern cities people are well educated and civilised.

'*The civilised cities is the lowest of the of all jungles, the only thing governing their morals is material possessions, recognition and fame. When a human being gains the world and loses himself in the process, he regresses back to the infantile stage where he becomes self absorbed, dismissive, and he yells when he does not get what he wants,*' The Chief replied.

'*Are you saying that living in the cities turns you into an animal?,*' One villager asked the chief .

'*Well if you give up your morals, your identity and your beliefs, then you will become something lower than an animal. Animals have a set of morals instilled in them, they only strive to survive and live by simple means; not to be recognised nor destroy,*' The Chief replied.

Few days later, the villagers gathered outside the fence to wish their fellow villager farewell. They jumped up and down singing a song named after the boy, now known as Fool. They all waved at him yelling, '*Bye Fool*'.

Years later, the boy returned with tears in his eyes, grey hair on his head and a naked back. He told the villagers his tale of unhappiness, loneliness from having no real friends and how mental illness caused by pressure to please broke his spirit.

The chief told him, '*You wanted to live it up, so you moved up by playing up and so they roughed you up simply because you jungled up. Now that you have woken up, grow up, fix up and keep your head up*'.

First Lesson For The Bird

Special

Friendship can be overrated
Relationships can be overrated
Love can be overrated
Food can be overrated
Items can be overrated
and those alike can also be overrated
Things are only highly rated
When genuine foundations are created
Discipline needs to be self dictated
then the amount & type can be weighted
This means the wasteful being vacated
and the blessings of life clearly stated
With the appreciation of life elated
Only then the special would be related.

Second Lesson For The bird

Redemption

The struggles of life can take a toll
It can leave us lost with an empty hole
What is existence without a purpose and goal?
Revelation begins with a self searching patrol
With righteousness guiding the body, mind and soul
The time has come to get back what the bygone days stole
Redemption is imperative for mankind to become whole.

Blissful life

Life, a precious gift we all share
We have no time to stand and stare
Free your mind from the loss of hope
The frustrations challenging one's ability to cope
Let go of the heavy burdens on your shoulders
The anger that turns us into scolders
Eradicate the pain that makes a heart numb
The loss, questioning a brighter future to come
Misfortunes can makes you wonder why
and tears can run your deep well dry
Worries you should not bear
Consult those around you who truly care
Leave fears behind at a place called yesterday
GOODBYE to the past, and here comes today
So cheers to a long life and a JOYFUL ONE
To those we call friends, the honest BLISSFUL ONES.

Confident Bird

See me for me

I want people to see me
For who I am
What I can do
But not for what I have
Because what I have
Will be here today
And gone the next day
So when I have nothing
It is me who remains
I may be down today
But I'll be up the next day
So watch me do what I do
And gain more than I lost
If I believe
If my mind conceives
Then I will achieve
I value me
Than things that are cheap
It is plain to see
That those who care for me
See me for me.

Happy Bird

Happiness

If it brings you down
And it makes your face frown
If something bad is said
Which hurts your head
If it feels wrong
Like you don't belong
If you lose sleep
Because you feel cheap
If you are pissed
Because they dismissed
If it isn't your fault
But it brings your world to a halt
Then flee the captivity
Happiness avoids negativity.

Positive Esteem

Impossible as it may seem
Reality is made out of dreams
What you need is a backing team
For your planned out scheme
So aim and focus your beam
To target a distant theme
You may encounter the extreme
When you swim upstream
To overcome the supreme
Remain positive in esteem.

The Bird's Letter To A Friend

Friendship

For when they are in doubt, we HOLD them
When in agony, we CONSOLE them
When confused, we rightly MOULD them
When wrong, we SCOLD them
With such care at hand, the walls of human nature won't restrain you forever.
When the obstacles of life inevitably crumble and an imminent bliss arrives, remember us like a beloved.

Yours sincerely

Friendship.

Changed Bird

For The Better

Less words, more action
Less complaining, more doing
Less preaching, more practising
Less hate, more compassion
Less greed, more deeds
Less ego, more humility
Less ignorance, more wisdom
Less following, more leading
Less for money, more 4 the spirit
Less fear, more bravery
Less grudges, more forgiving
Less envy, more inspirations
Less tears, more cheers
Less surrender, more dreaming
Less haste, more patience
Less foulness, more realness
Less time wasting, more living it up
Why settle for less, when you can do more?
With more, the world within and without would be a peaceful and happier place.

Bird In Control

Stay Positively Alive (SPA)

Care less without being careless
Fear less without being fearless
Hope less without being hopeless
Hear less without being earless
Speak less without being speechless
Sleep less without being sleepless
Love less without being loveless
Need less without being needless
Be in control without being out of control

Stay strong, stay positive, stay Alive.

Revolutionary Bird

Fight back

Those who have the power to rule
See those below as mere tools
Since the ancient times
They have been committing crimes
While we are killing one another
We forget that we are blood brothers
Did you ever stop to think
How life passes by in a blink?
While we act foolish and fight
They sit comfortably with delight
Life is a game to be played
But fear makes us easily swayed
Even though we bleed through similar veins
Hate and darkness easily possess our brains
Some have nothing to claim
But they brag and flaunt with no shame
Freedom requires the mind to be tamed
So think before you point fingers and blame
What we need is the will to be brave
and the right character in the way we behave

When the road gets rough and sends us off track
All we need to do is stand up and fight back.

World Experience Of The Bird

Did they think you don't hurt too?

Being nice takes effort
Being nice requires energy
Against all odds you remain strong
People will assume you're a walk over
Not knowing it takes courage
Being angry, anyone can do
Being frustrated, anyone can be
Being judgemental, anyone can display
People will point out your faults
And dismiss your strengths
'*You're naive,*' they would say
'*You're soft,*' they would utter
Not knowing it is you who is brave
Didn't they know humility is inner peace?
While hostility is internal turmoil
Being nice takes effort
Being nice requires energy
Against all odds your remained strong
When they do push your buttons too far
When they do cross a line

And you tell them the truth
About the person behind the mask
The one you've known all this while
Feelings would get hurt
They would now scream out foul
Did they forget about their insensitive actions?
Now they know being nice takes effort
Being nice takes courage
Against all odds you remained strong
Nice people are living beings too
Did they think you don't hurt too?

Bird's Letter To The Doubters

Dear Mistaken

Remember the lack of care in your joyous glory
Remember the lack of sincerity in your beautiful story
Remember the lack of wisdom in the decisions you made
Remember the lack of mercy as you dug in the blade
Remember the lack of humanity as you laughed loudly
Remember the lack of empathy as you stood proudly
Remember the lack of friendship in your deceptive kindness
Remember the lack of heart in your ways of blindness
Remember the lack of gratitude you may not mend
Remember the lack of compassion when it all ends
In the end, you should have known better
In the end, the sorrow felt as you read the letter
In the end, you stare at the stones you have been busy collecting
In the end, you value the diamonds you have been neglecting
In the end, karma came by and got you checked
In the end, you ended up wrecked
In the end, you question your naive quickness
In the end, you are on bended knees pleading for forgiveness
In the end, all that is golden has been taken
In the end, you are only remembered as mistaken.

A Cold Bird

Winter Warmth

Winter came and froze my soul
But you walked in and I became whole
Winter came and stole the sun
But your presence brought colour and fun
Winter came and I lost sight
But your spirit became an illuminating light
Winter came and I felt nude
But with your embrace I am renewed
Winter came and I caught a cold
But with your care I feel like gold
Winter came and made me shiver
But calmness is what a rose delivers
Winter came and It was a bitter storm
But you made it exquisitely warm.

Bird's Choice; Summer or Winter?

The One

One is an easy find, the other is one of a kind
One looks good, the other sounds beautiful
One plays minds, the other explores minds
One loves the mirror, the other loves her future
One men change, the other changes a man
One is a man's treat, the other a man keeps
One sits and looks, the other loves to cook
One love slacks, the other loves back
One is a mind-shock, the other a diamond rock
One is worth losing, the other is worth fighting for
One is just a girl, the other a definite Queen.

Rational Bird

A Diamonds Worth

A diamond is invisible to the blind
which makes it a difficult find
The rock is found in the midst of dirt
unable to glisten nor alert
The believers who mould it
go out of their way to hold it
Its charm is the soulful mirrors within
which radiates through the outer skin
Shallow minds may be now impressed
when they notice the exquisitely blessed
Replicas imitate the imperial rock
But the phony will give you a heart-shock
So before celebrating as a czar
Be sure to have found a shooting star
The extraordinary has no twin
because a diamond's worth is found within.

Confession Of A Bird

Unconditional Love

When I was lost
You found me
When I had nothing
You stuck around me
When I was down
You lifted me high
When I was out of touch
You didn't judge me sly
When I acted a fool
You schooled me
When I was angered
You cooled me
When I was hurtful
You forgave me
When I wanted freedom
You didn't enslave me.

I fly high above
with your unconditional Love.

The Stubborn Bird

Sometimes

Sometimes I want to erase you but yet I think of you
Sometimes you annoy me but yet I miss you
Sometimes I dislike you but yet I yearn to kiss you
Sometimes I aim to replace you but yet nothing is as good as you
Sometimes I curse you but yet I praise you
Sometimes I turn to frowns but yet you turn me into smiles
Sometimes you frustrate me but yet I crave to converse with you
Sometimes I can wait no longer but with your touch I become patient.

The truth is, "sometimes" is how special you are to me.
The day you are gone is when "sometimes" becomes "all the time".
Before that happens, make those you care for feel special most of the time.

Preaching Bird

Good Relations

While we fuss and fight
What have we gained?
While we cuss and fright
What have we obtained?
While we act nuts and bite
Has our spirit been stained?
Without the will to discuss and acting right
How can we be explained?
With deaf ears and no sight
How else can understanding be ascertained?
Maturity means respect and being forthright
This is how good relations are maintained.

Bird In Love

The Nature Of Love

Birds were not created to be on their own
From birth we yearn for love as if it's our home
Loving relationships, more joyful than troublesome
Like an addict never to be on your lonesome
Memories of the tosses and turns, the sleepless nights
Whether it is excitement or worries, it feels so right
Days of a single life are memories far gone
Now an item, were you ever alone?
The stares, the giggles, a kiss under the shining moon
Poetry in motion, will it be over too soon?
Roller-coaster rides of ups and downs
Cycles of smiles, cheers and frowns
A flight to cloud nine, high up above
Does anything compare to the nature of LOVE?

Proposition Of A Bird

Revelation

As I begin to reflect, my mind paces back and forth
With comprehension comes discernment henceforth
Vivid pictures of togetherness flash before my eyes
An epiphany reminds one that blindness was unwise
Through ignorance we misconstrue intentions of sincerity
As I reminisce, your touch was truly a rarity
From here on, sweet love and care is the way onwards
No more fights, romance shall be straightforward
Visions of you and I have never been so crystal clear
Your unconditional love is visible through a tear
Through endless worries I can feel your pain
Try to understand we are not all the same
The only girl in the world, my expression to you
Dreams of eternity nothing more than true
Actions speak louder so I am on bended knees
I pop the question with a nerve raking please
These aren't just words nor flirtation
Forever more as my summer breeze is the revelation.

Smile

What will be of tomorrow?
Will it be euphoria or sorrow?
Living will come with struggle
But still continue with the hustle
When you've been through life's puzzles
It grows you bigger back muscles
That's when the soul begins to worry less
which makes you fear less
No matter the situation remain humble
Even when you go through a fumble
So fasten your seatbelt with style
And take on the road with a smile.

Smile today, tomorrow and forever.

Two Face

The chosen one with a classified mission
"*At all cost*" is the secretive ambition
He prowls the streets with a sharp dagger
An assassin with a smooth swagger
With sharp claws concealed in gestures of kindness
He captures the victim with emotive methods of blindness
Specialised in the art of masking his face
An agenda articulated with pure grace
He's known for uttering soothing words
Like the deceptive sounds of mockingbirds
To the victim, "what a friend"
To the gossip hungry, a means to an end
The truth of fact, call it life
How can one see those with a hidden knife?
In the circle of existence, sincerity is bliss
And bitter resentment most dismiss
So be watchful of those who you embrace
Some are known as Two Face.

The Beauty Of Your Soul

The smile on your face
Moves the world with effortless grace
The twinkle in your eyes
Electrifies hearts to new highs
The warmth of your touch
Wipes away fears so much
The good intentions you display
Uplifts those gone astray
So as you walk through the darkest night
Let your spirit be a beacon of light
Ignite the world ablaze
With unconditional happy days
You're a shining star that makes the world whole
Simply because of the beauty of your soul.

Dedicated to the bird's mother.

Wise Bird

See Clear

To see light
Seek insight
To think right
Muster your might
To act polite
Never spite
To feel delight
Cast away your frights
To avoid foolish fights
Make others feel alright
To be respected like a knight
Always be forthright
To love another outright
Stand brave in tall height
To sleep well at night
Have future hopes in flight
To grow bright
See past the obvious black & white.

The Bird Mentors

Why women are complex

When a woman loves a guy, she does it with all her heart. She would dream of him, she would wake up for him, she looks forward to seeing him, she would pick a dress with matching shoes for him, she would do her makeup and hair for him, she would talk about him and at night she can't sleep because of him.

A woman would do all these complex things and more for a man, which would make her behaviour appear complex. All it takes is simple compliments of her hair, her dress and a mere mention of what she has done for you.

Hold her hand when she's insecure, *hug her* when she wants attention and *romance* her when she's jealous. Women are hard work but if you want your end of the bargain then you should do your part. If you do, just sit back and watch how she would do anything because her heart is filled with happiness.

She plays games to make you feel as *she feels* or to encourage you to *step up* or to truly understand *who you are.*. At the end of the day, she has a lot to lose, physically and emotionally.

Do not take her too seriously, at times show a fun patient side and at other times let her know of the things you do not condone.

As a men we need be to firm, principled and draw a line but pride serves no purpose other than to evoke a negative reaction. Women are like the weather, one day they are *sunny*, the next *rainy*, the other *cold* and the next its *thunder*. If you want constant sunshine, open your eyes and be on your toes. If it's rainy, you should fetch an umbrella and sing a song. If it's cold, you should cuddle and warm her up. If it's thundery, give the storm (her) some space.

In the end, nothing but her love for you will calm her down. Choose which battles you fight, not all are fought in the same way or need fighting at all. They are not perfect but they will take care of us perfectly if we play our cards right! Don't get mad if another man has your woman, he did what you were not.

To be fair, not all women are angels, some are selfish and unappreciative. I'm talking about *good women*, so choose which one is worth fighting for.

Bird Reflects On Life

A Place Called Home

Vivid pictures have me reminiscing
Flashing thoughts of what I've been missing
I wonder, how long will I last?
Counting years as time blasts
I've seen passions faded
Lost souls in agony while intoxicated
As I'm out here in the world alone
I contemplate my departure from home
The trials and tribulations
Yearned for answers and explanations
With pressing thoughts came reflection
What of existence without caring affection?
I am told life is a tale of love and longing
Picture countless without a place of belonging
While the world dreams of material wealth
I've been ruminating of inner spiritual health
Family times is what we leave behind
A precious dime that has been heavy on my mind
Yeah, I've been gone for a while
But these revelations have me flashing smiles

The writing on the wall now says this
'Unconditional love is eternal bliss'
As I return to my throne of living
My hands hold a gift worth giving
I now find myself in a happy zone
As I arrive at a place called home.

A Legend Is Born

The Eagle

Have you seen the bird in the sky?
It sees all from the high
With a sharp zoom
It senses peace and doom
But those without wings
Mock the one who sings
As fools bark at a flying bird
Whispers are what it heard
So it landed from flight
And brought fear with its might
The absurd scattered fast
And he who won laughed last
Reality became an offence
To those who have no sense
But the rumours did spread
Of the ruler they should dread
And so the kingdom bowed down
To the one wearing the crown
It returned to the air
glaring at giants in a scare

Now they know what wisdom brings
The flying eagle is the king of kings.

A Slave Of Self

When they are above you
They look down on you
When you're on your way up
They ignore you
When you've made it to the top
They praise you
When you're living well
They judge you
When you make a mistake
They laugh at you
When you lose it all
They are happy that you are down
When you're a nobody
They dismiss you
When you're dead and buried
They feel sorry for you

Instead of allowing the failure or success of someone to determine your treatment, let it inspire you to be better in every way.

When somebody is down, lift them up. When somebody is high, hold them up. You'd be surprised how positivity would take you far in life in terms of motivation, growth, opportunity, progress, peace of mind, good sleep and good health. It is a shame that most of us allow the darkness to creep in because of our current position in life; we accept the present emotional comfort since we cannot envision our own future. Be who you want to be, don't be a slave of your own self or what others make you out to be.

The Circle Of Life

CREATION is for those who turn dreams into reality
CHANGE is for those who take a chance on the new
HAPPINESS is for those who find inner peace and tranquillity
LOVE is for those willing to sacrifice self
FRIENDSHIP is for those who are there through the darkest night
TRUST is the willingness to believe
EXPERIENCE is for those who try and learn
FAMILY is for those who will always be connected
SPIRITUALITY is finding meaning of inner self
WISDOM is the awareness of the circle of life.
SUCCESS is for those who turn any of these into reality.
GREATNESS is for those willing to dream big
LEGACY is for those who have moved minds and touched hearts.
LIFE is the will to live to the fullest, every second, minute and hour.

Life Of Valuable Emotions (L.O.V.E)

Love is the ultimate force that can change and move mountains. Whether its humbly loving yourself, loving life, loving your faith, loving friends, loving that special someone, loving your bloodline or simply showing love to the helpless or lost, there is nothing as powerful or as potent to the soul.

They say you have to go through dirt to get to the good part. For most, life is a 360 degree journey from an infant screaming out for tender love and care to adolescent experiences of disappointments, distrust and numbness; to adulthood in search of meaning and understanding. When you do experience any kind of goodness, the circle of life will swing back to LOVE.

So find something worth loving , worth dreaming about, worth looking forward to and most importantly stay alive in this road we call life.

The Mission

Are you a bird in a cage?

Or

A bird from the golden age, flying high like a sage?

You are on stage,

So pick up a pen and write it on histories page.

www.ingramcontent.com/pod-product-compliance
Ingram Content Group UK Ltd.
Pitfield, Milton Keynes, MK11 3LW, UK
UKHW020233250726
13967UKWH00001B/344

9 781291 639278